SCHOLASTIC

create and display

Performing Arts

Full of exciting activities and displays for the whole curriculum

Ages 5-11

Céline George and Rebecca Bruce

SCHOLASTIC

Book End, Range Road, Witney, Oxfordshire, OX29 OYD
www.scholastic.co.uk

1 2 3 4 5 6 7 8 9   0 1 2 3 4 5 6 7 8 9

British Library Cataloguing-in-Publication Data
A catalogue record for this book is available from the British Library.

ISBN 978-1407-12530-5
Printed by Bell & Bain Ltd, Glasgow

Commissioning Editor
Paul Naish

Development Editor
Emily Jefferson

Editor
Tracy Kewley

Series Designer and Cover Design
Andrea Lewis and Sarah Garbett

Designers
Sonja Bagley and Liz Gilbert

Photography
Steve Forrest

FSC www.fsc.org MIX Paper from responsible sources FSC® C007785

Acknowledgements

The authors would like to thank all the staff and children of Hilden Grange School for their wonderful work in the Performing Arts, and extend a special thanks to the children on the editorial team of the school magazine for their enthusiasm and help. The authors would like to thank the Royal Academy of Arts cReAte Programme and Peter Feroze for their inspirational work. They would like to thank Gavin Bruce, Christopher Cole, Sophie George and Maggie Hewson for their expert help, and Jo Clutton for co-writing the story *One and Two Halves to Buckingham Palace*. A special thank you to John Withers for his enthusiastic support and encouragement, and to Dianne Dartnell for her creative inspiration and for co-writing the story *Sunil and Sunita*. Finally, the authors would like to thank Chris Cox and Charlotte Parker for their gracious and expert help at all times and for outstanding work in the Performing Arts.

The Publishers would like to thank:

Musicline Publications and Craig Hawes for allowing us to use the play *What a Knight!* as a case study (www.musiclinedirect.com)

Andrew Holdsworth for creation of Indian-themed music (CD-ROM only).

Images
Page 12, Mehandi © Sunil Kumar/istockphoto; Peacock © think4photop/shutterstock; page 17, Nelson's Column © Andrew Nokes/istockphoto; Big Ben © Sergey Borisov/istockphoto; London bus © Christopher Steer/istockphoto; page 23, London Bridge © TonyMarinella/istockphoto, page 29, Tea party © Tammy Bryngelson/istockphoto

Contents

Introduction

Create and Display: Performing Arts uses paintings, stories, poetry, urban art, playscripts, dance performances, journalistic writing and everyday objects as starting points for working creatively within the Performing Arts. The aim of the book is to demonstrate how to use a range of inspirational art forms to promote creativity. The chapters cover a variety of skills all linked to performance, including drawing, landscape painting, dance performance, portrait paintings, performance poetry, textile paintings and creative writing. The book offers new ideas for using the work of famous artists such as Banksy, Keith Haring, David Hockney, René Magritte, Paul Klee, Andy Warhol and Paul Rubens, with a focus on the Performing Arts.

Throughout the book, we talk about offering children the chance to attend professional performances and use artists' work as an inspirational starting point. Inviting local artists into the classroom can add a sense of excitement and an extra element of motivation for the children. There may even be parents or friends of the school who can contribute their expertise. During the writing of this book, we liaised with the educational department at the Royal Academy of Art and they worked with us on a variety of drawing activities. The children were very focused during the activities and produced some amazing quick-fire drawings and highly imaginative landscape paintings.

Contents

Introduction

Create and Display: Performing Arts uses paintings, stories, poetry, urban art, playscripts, dance performances, journalistic writing and everyday objects as starting points for working creatively within the Performing Arts. The aim of the book is to demonstrate how to use a range of inspirational art forms to promote creativity. The chapters cover a variety of skills all linked to performance, including drawing, landscape painting, dance performance, portrait paintings, performance poetry, textile paintings and creative writing. The book offers new ideas for using the work of famous artists such as Banksy, Keith Haring, David Hockney, René Magritte, Paul Klee, Andy Warhol and Paul Rubens, with a focus on the Performing Arts.

Throughout the book, we talk about offering children the chance to attend professional performances and use artists' work as an inspirational starting point. Inviting local artists into the classroom can add a sense of excitement and an extra element of motivation for the children. There may even be parents or friends of the school who can contribute their expertise. During the writing of this book, we liaised with the educational department at the Royal Academy of Art and they worked with us on a variety of drawing activities. The children were very focused during the activities and produced some amazing quick-fire drawings and highly imaginative landscape paintings.

Some of the chapters in this book refer to texts written by teachers. These are available for you to use in class on the companion CD-ROM, *Create and Display Interactive: Performing Arts* but you could also write your own stories or poems and use them as starting points for the activities. It is important that you use starting points that inspire you. For example, we looked at the work of the street artist Banksy as an example of how contemporary practitioners can provide a new and interesting approach to project work.

All of the projects in the book are suitable for use in the classroom but some could also be used in after-school art, drama or creative writing clubs, perhaps using a cross-curricular approach. It is important to emphasise the value of working collaboratively with colleagues especially during the process of putting on a performance, from planning and preparation to the final show.

Throughout this book, there are references to 'Ideas books'. These are drawing books that contain children's sketches, designs and notes. They are invaluable to their creative experience and will become a vibrant record of all their ideas throughout the year.

Céline George and Rebecca Bruce

Creative Arts Week

Many schools have already discovered the importance of putting creativity at the centre of all teaching and learning. One strategy that can be used across the school and that encompasses all the Arts is to hold a Creative Arts Week. During the week, children should be introduced to a wide range of art forms and given opportunities to experiment with a variety of objects, materials and themes. This increases their interest in the Arts and allows them to use personal experience as a learning tool. A Creative Arts Week is a time when the structure of the day, teaching styles and community involvement inevitably take centre stage. The opportunity to enjoy diverse activities and concentrate on simple themes not only benefits the children but also enables the teaching staff to reflect on their own practice.

Day 1

The examples in this chapter focus around a Creative Arts Week based on the theme of 'Colours of India'. This is just one example of the many themes that could be used – the ideas can be easily adapted to suit your own theme or topic. To prepare for Creative Arts Week, choose a suitable story to base your work around. You may wish to write your own, as was done for the work shown in this chapter, where a specially written story called *Sunil and Sunita* was used to inspire children's creativity. The vibrant colours of India were reflected in a set of book illustrations drawn by children to depict different aspects of the story. These illustrations were then used as a stimulus for further creative work.

The Memory Box

Begin the week by inviting an Indian dancer to demonstrate a variety of dance movements in school assembly. At the end of the performance, ask the dancer to present the children with a jewelled box and explain that she had been asked to give it to children who love music, art and dancing. The children will be intrigued. The scene can be enhanced by playing Indian music in the background.

Resources

- Indian music
- Small cardboard boxes
- Paint brushes
- Gold or silver metallic poster paint
- Some examples of traditional Indian designs and patterns
- Collage materials such as sequins, jewels and coloured paper
- PVA glue and spreaders
- Scissors
- Hand-made paper

Approach

1 Play a piece of Indian music softly and remind the children of the jewelled box that the dancer presented to them earlier.

2 Ask the children to paint their cardboard boxes inside and out with the metallic paints and leave to dry for a couple of hours.

3 Show the children some traditional Indian designs and patterns and ask them to decorate their boxes in an Indian style with a variety of sequins, jewels and coloured paper.

4 As an additional piece of work, ask the children to use their imaginations to create a poem starting with the line: 'Inside my box I would like to find…' Transfer the poems to scrolls made from hand-made paper and place them in the memory boxes as treasure.

Day 2

Create a sense of awe by displaying a range of Indian artefacts in the school hall. Include the memory boxes that the children have already designed and made. Play some Indian music and exhibit any illustrations you have prepared to go with your chosen story. Encourage the children and staff to wear Indian costumes to set the scene. Read your chosen story. (If you are using a different theme, you can use any published story that supports your chosen theme, or write your own.)

Indian Elephant Prints

Elephants are important symbols in Indian culture. If you are covering a different theme it is important to select an image, object, animal, pattern or other symbol that is equally well suited to your theme.

Resources

- Ideas books
- Polystyrene tiles (about 16cm x 12cm)
- Blunt pencils or biros
- Water-based black printing ink
- Printing rollers
- Mulberry or hand-made paper in vibrant colours (about 16cm x 12cm)
- A4 card
- Examples of Indian designs and patterns
- Metallic pens or pencils
- Sketching pencils
- Glue sticks

Approach

1. Ask the children to draw a simple elephant shape in their Ideas books, then to transfer the shape onto a polystyrene tile by pressing a blunt pencil or biro onto the surface.
2. Demonstrate how to make a print. Roll the ink onto the surface of the tile, then place the mulberry paper over the inked tile and press down. Peel the paper off and leave to dry.
3. Let the children make their prints.
4. When the prints are dry, the children should stick them onto card and create an Indian border design using the metallic pens or pencils around the edge of the coloured card.

Flower Paintings

Flowers painted in a suitable style can be used to decorate walls, classrooms or other areas to give an Indian feel. Use vibrant coloured flowers as an inspiration and paint them using a combination of chalk pastels and Indian ink.

Resources

- Flowers or photographs of flowers
- A3 sketch paper
- Indian ink
- Chalk pastels

Approach

1. Ask the children to make careful observations of flowers.
2. Invite them to use chalk pastels and Indian ink to create vibrant flower paintings.

Lotus Flower Tealights

The lotus flower conveys a real sense of Indian culture, and creating tealight holders in a lotus flower shape can help to add an Indian feel to any performance.

Resources

- Tealights (battery-powered versions are available)
- Air-drying clay
- Wooden boards
- Clay tools
- Brushes
- Acrylic paints
- PVA glue

Approach

1. Tell the children that they are going to create a tealight holder in the shape of a lotus flower using a single piece of clay.
2. Take a small ball of clay and a wooden board and show the children how to stretch the clay to form petals. Allow space for a tealight to be placed in the centre.
3. Let the children make their flowers. They can create texture and add details by using clay tools to score into the clay. Leave the flowers to dry naturally.
4. Invite the children to paint their flowers using thick acrylic paint, choosing the vivid colours of India.
5. When they are dry, coat the flowers with PVA glue.
6. As a final touch, place the tealights in the centre.

Day 3

Invite some Indian drummers or other musicians to give an exciting performance at the start of the day. You could also visit a suitable cultural location such as a Sikh temple. This will inspire children's ideas as they will see examples of intricate Rangoli patterns and other beautiful designs from the temples and palaces of India. Music and dance workshops are also great ways to help children develop and express themselves.

Ganesh Stories

Encourage the children to write their own stories inspired by the story of Ganesh, the god of new beginnings. Read the story to the children as a starting point.

Resources

- An illustrated version of the Ganesh story, for example, *How Ganesh Got His Elephant Head* by Harish Johari, Vatsala Sperling and Pieter Weltevrede (Bear Cub Books, 2003)
- Storyboard templates with spaces for illustration and text
- Pens or pencils

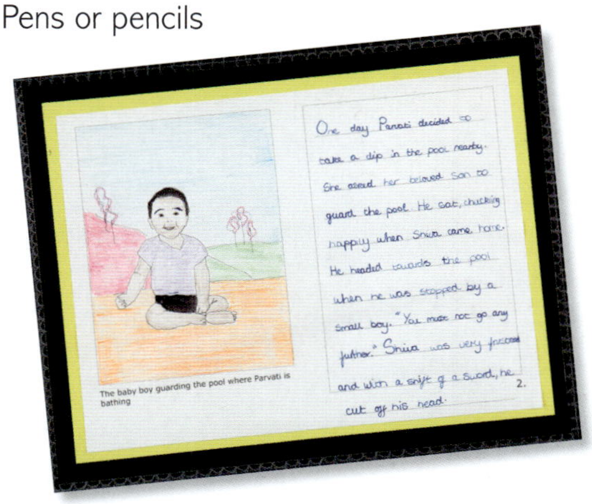

Approach

1. Divide the children into groups of four and ask each group to create their own storyboard illustrations for the story beginning, middle, resolution and ending.
2. Re-read the story and discuss the stunning start, marvellous middle and fantastic finish with the children. Use the techniques of prediction, visualisation and empathy to explore the deeper meaning of the story.
3. Ask each child to write one of the sections on a storyboard template so that each group of four will have a complete story at the end of the session. Give the groups time to read and revise their stories together, then encourage them to read their stories aloud to the rest of the class.

Fabric Elephants

In many traditional Indian stories, elephants are draped in wonderfully decorated fabrics embellished with gold and silver threads. This activity involves making fabric elephants using a variety of vibrant coloured materials to add texture and to reflect an Indian scene.

Resources

- Images of decorated Indian elephants
- Elephant templates on card
- Rectangles of hessian material frayed at the edges and big enough to accommodate the elephant template
- Brightly coloured felt
- Scissors
- PVA glue
- Scraps of fabric
- Sequins
- Glitter glue
- Feathers
- Coloured card

Approach

1 Show the children images of decorated Indian elephants. Talk about how the elephant is draped with highly decorative cloths embellished with gold and silver threads.

2 Invite the children to choose a piece of felt, then to draw round the elephant template on the felt and cut it out.

3 They can then stick the felt elephant shape onto the hessian background with PVA glue and embellish the elephant using a variety of fabric, sequins, glitter glue and feathers.

4 Finally, ask the children to glue the hessian onto a piece of coloured card.

5 Display the fabric elephants together as a wall-hanging.

Day 4

Begin the day by offering children a variety of practical workshops. These could include creating their own henna hand designs and making vibrant paintings of the peacock, the national bird of India.

Henna Hands

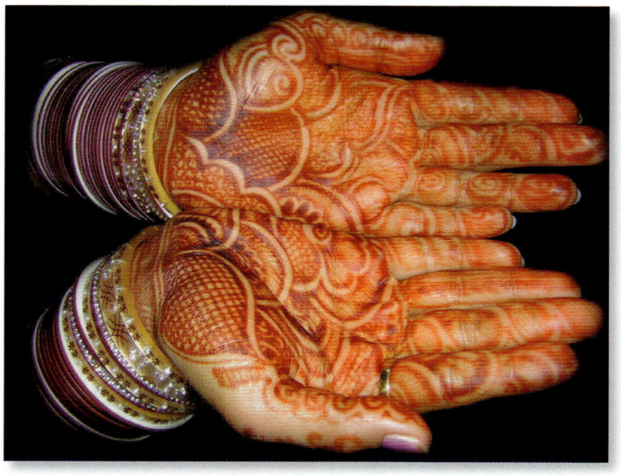

Resources

- Images of henna hands
- Coloured card
- Sketching pencils and rubbers
- Fine, brown felt pens

Approach

1. Begin by looking at images of henna hand designs and discuss the different patterns.
2. Ask the children to draw round their own hands in pencil onto the card.
3. Invite them to create a pattern reaching up each finger, using light pencil strokes and starting with the central palm design.
4. When they are happy with their design, they can use fine, brown felt-tipped pens to go over the pencil lines.
5. The pencil lines can be rubbed out when the pen is dry.

Peacock Paintings

Resources

- Peacock template
- Colouring pencils
- Sketching pencils
- Metallic pens
- Images of peacocks
- Coloured card
- Rubbers
- Good quality white paper

Approach

1. Create a peacock template, using images from books or the internet to help you.
2. Give out copies of the template and ask the children to draw in the detail of the peacock's feathers, using images of peacocks to help them.
3. Encourage them to use different shades of green and blue pencil to add colour. Metallic pens could also be used to good effect.
4. Finally, invite the children to draw in the peacock's face and colour its body.
5. Mount the children's work on coloured card.

Story Openings

Ask the children to write group story openings based on images from *Sunil and Sunita*, or your chosen story. You could also use any of the images you have created with them throughout the week as the basis for a story opening. Inviting the children to read their story openings aloud will enhance both their confidence and enjoyment of this creative writing activity.

Resources

- Examples of powerful story openings in illustrated books
- Illustrations from the story *Sunil and Sunita* (*Create and Display Interactive: Performing Arts*) or any suitable themed story
- Pens or pencils
- Ideas books

Approach

1 Look through the books in school to find a few examples of powerful story openings in illustrated books. Read these to the children and discuss their effect on the reader.

2 Show the children the first three illustrations from the story *Sunil and Sunita*, or another story of your choice, and explain to the children that they are going to use them as a starting point for creative writing. Tell them that they should aim for a stunning opening that will hook the reader in and grab their attention straight away.

3 Divide the children into three groups and ask them to work collaboratively to write a plan for a story opening linked closely to the book illustrations (if possible, using an adult as scribe).

4 Working from their plans, ask the children to write a short but effective group story opening (again, using an adult as scribe, if possible).

5 Ask one child from each group to read their story opening to the class audience and encourage the children to comment on their own work and the work of others.

6 As an additional piece of work, the children could finish their group story using the rest of the book illustrations as inspiration.

Example story opening:

Deep in a quiet village, bordering the River Ganges, there lived two poor children named Rashid and Meena. The sun gleamed and smiled down on the villagers as turquoise, orange and purple saris rustled and swirled to the beat of the drum. Jewellery jangled. It was a special day and women and children joined in the celebrations. In the distance, the deafening sound of rampaging elephants stirred the dust towards the town…

Day 5

Taj Mahal Display

The Taj Mahal is probably the most famous Indian building, and is an iconic symbol of India across the world. It was built by Shah Jahan, the Mughal Emperor, between 1632 and 1653, and is a mausoleum to his wife Mumtaz Mahal. It is seen as a symbol of the Emperor's great love for his wife, and is an excellent subject for any study or performance covering India.

Resources

- A3 sketch paper
- Watercolour paints in vibrant colours
- Paint brushes
- Paper plates for mixing paint
- A simple outline drawing of the Taj Mahal on A4 paper
- Pink and cream A4 sketch paper
- Fine line black pens
- White chalk pastels
- Scissors
- Gold and silver pens
- Glue sticks

Approach

1 Give the children sheets of A3 sketch paper and ask them to add paint in strips of vibrant colours. Leave to dry.
2 Photocopy the drawing of the Taj Mahal onto pink or cream A4 sketch paper and give each child a copy.
3 Ask the children to add detail to the drawing with a fine line pen and white chalk pastels. They could also embellish it with gold and silver pens.
4 Children can then cut out their Taj Mahal image and stick it to the middle of the A3 painted sheet.
5 Place the paintings together to create a display that reflects the colours of India.

The Colours of India Performance

A performance incorporating story, mime, drama, music and dance is a fitting end to a Creative Arts Week. In an Indian-themed week, Bhangra is an excellent choice, and your performance could be choreographed to tell the story that you've been working on. You will need to practise Bhangra movement and dance several weeks before the actual performance. (Invite a Bhangra dancer to help you, or search online for suitable videos.) Ensure that each child is offered the opportunity to participate in the dances; this means careful consideration when choreographing the different routines. During the performance, project the illustrations from your story behind the dancers, so that the children can use the projected illustrations as their cue. The story could end with a jubilant Bollywood feel, with music such as *Jai Ho* or something equally vibrant.

Resources

- Indian music, including *Jai Ho*
- Indian costumes and jewellery
- Copy of *Sunil and Sunita* (*Create and Display Interactive: Performing Arts*) or any suitable themed story
- Props linked to your chosen story
- Children's artwork from the week
- Projector

Approach

1 Set the scene by playing a piece of contemporary Indian music. A track such as *Jai Ho* will inspire the children as they will probably have heard it before. Display one of the illustrations from your story and invite a small group of children to form a frozen tableau of the scene.

2 Explain to the class that they are going to tell the story through mime, drama, music and dance.

3 In an open space, slowly narrate the story and ask the children to mime the actions of the story. Work with the class to decide which of the mimes are strongest and should be used in the performance. You will also need to decide who will play the key parts.

4 The performance of the story should stop at intervals to include the practised dance routines, and there should be cues in the story narration to introduce the dances.

5 During the performance, display artwork that the children have made during the week to enhance the scene and celebrate their achievements.

6 Take photographs during the performance and ask the children to take a bow after the last dance.

Creative Literacy Week

A week devoted to developing children's writing skills is well worth embarking on. When children's writing is closely linked with exciting activities within the Performing Arts, their confidence is enhanced and they often excel. A few weeks before starting the project, look at illustrated stories, including ones with minimal text and discuss the importance of the images with the children.

As an inspiration for the week's work, this chapter uses the story, *One and Two Halves to Buckingham Palace*, written by two teachers. The setting for the example in this chapter is London in the 1950s. In the story, two children go on a special outing with their mother to visit Buckingham Palace. Travelling by bus, they see many landmark buildings and signs of celebrations along the way. When they finally arrive at their destination, things don't work out exactly as planned!

The story *One and Two Halves to Buckingham Palace* is available to use in *Create and Display Interactive: Performing Arts* but it could be an excellent idea to work with the children and other teachers to write your own story so that it is something suited to your school and pupils.

London Sketches

Resources

- Photographs of landmark buildings and London scenes (such as Buckingham Palace, Big Ben, Trafalgar Square, St Paul's Cathedral, a London bus)
- A3 sketch paper
- Sketching pencils
- Crayons and colouring pencils

Approach

1. Look at a variety of photographs of landmark London buildings and discuss their significance with the children.
2. Working individually, ask the children to sketch a favourite London scene or building.
3. Invite them to add colour with crayons or colouring pencils.

A Taste of London

Launch your Creative Literacy Week with an assembly to introduce the theme of 'An Exciting Day Out'. A PowerPoint® presentation showing a selection of vivid images of landmark buildings in London, both now and in the 1950s, would work well for the example story. Tell the children that they are going to bring a story to life with their drawings. Alternatively, you can write your own story.

Resources

- The story *One and Two Halves to Buckingham Palace* (*Create and Display Interactive: Performing Arts*) or story ideas based on a real day out, for example, a recent school excursion
- Photos of London landmarks including Big Ben and Westminster Bridge, Trafalgar Square and Nelson's Column, Buckingham Palace
- Photos or videos of the Queen's coronation and the wedding of the Duke and Duchess of Cambridge, both in Westminster Abbey
- Photos of Prince Charles and Princess Anne as young children and more recent images
- Photos of children visiting London in the 1950s (teachers or parents could provide old family photographs taken in the 1950s)
- Five A3-sized photographs showing a 1950s red bus, Big Ben, pigeons in Trafalgar Square, Buckingham Palace and the Queen on the balcony at her coronation
- Five sheets of A3 card
- Glue

Approach

1 In a school assembly, use PowerPoint® to show a range of images and videos of London, now and during the 1950s. Try to include footage from the Queen's coronation in 1953 and footage from a recent royal event, such as the marriage of the Duke and Duchess of Cambridge.

2 Look at buildings in London that are mentioned in the story *One and Two Halves to Buckingham Palace.*

3 Before reading the story, make some story photo cards by dividing the text into five A3- sized pages and then sticking each one onto A3 card. Put photographs linked to the text on the other side. You can then easily hold up the card with a matching image on the other side so that children can follow the story more easily.

4 In class, read the story *One and Two Halves to Buckingham Palace* with the children and mention that the story is based on a national event that actually happened: the Queen's coronation in 1953. Explain that this was an exciting event that the whole country celebrated. Compare the celebration to the recent marriage of the Duke and Duchess of Cambridge, where people flocked to London to be part of the celebrations.

One and Two Halves to Buckingham Palace

The activities on the following pages are divided into themes, each linking with a part of the story *One and Two Halves to Buckingham Palace:* 'A Bus Journey' (pages 20–21), 'A View from the Bridge' (pages 22–23), 'Admiral Nelson and the Pigeons' (pages 24–25), 'A Visit to the Palace' (pages 26–27), and 'A London Scene' (pages 28–29). For each part of the story, children create collaborative class displays reflecting the relevant piece of text. Read through the story and focus on sections from the text that conjure up vivid images. It is important that the children create their own illustrations. As part of the activities for Creative Literacy Week, you could also look at a selection of nursery rhymes, poems and songs that link with the themes of the story. Finally, why not introduce dance and music to enhance the final performance of the story and make children's experience of the Creative Arts a highly enjoyable one?

Book Illustration Displays

A good way to actively involve the children in the telling of the story is to create large classroom displays to be used as book illustrations. As these take time, it would make sense for different classes to each focus on a separate display. Getting every child involved in this process is important, so working on a big board ensures that everyone has an input.

Resources

- Large MDF boards
- Emulsion paint
- Tissue paper in various colours
- Poster paint
- Paint brushes
- Images of London landmarks
- A variety of illustrated children's stories

Approach

1 Look at a variety of children's stories and focus on the illustrations and how they are linked closely to the text.

2 Give each class a different theme from the story *One and Two Halves to Buckingham Palace* to work from.

3 Explain to the children that they are going to create a display that will be used as one of the illustrations in the story.

4 If possible, take the children on a school trip to London and focus on one or two landmark buildings linked closely to the theme they are working on.

A Bus Journey

At the beginning of the story *One and Two Halves to Buckingham Palace*, the two children, Alice and Nicholas, travel to London on a red bus. During their journey, they pass many iconic buildings and enjoy the sights of London from their excellent viewpoint at the top of the bus. Encourage the children to make their own London bus with 3D faces peering out from the windows. This project is ideal for younger children.

Big Red Bus

Resources

- Large MDF board
- White emulsion paint
- White and blue tissue paper
- PVA glue and brushes
- Black and white poster paint
- Sand
- Paint brushes
- Image of a red London bus in the 1950s
- Sketching pencil
- Staple gun

Approach

1 Paint one side of MDF board with white emulsion paint and leave to dry.
2 Place the board in the landscape position.
3 Draw a horizontal line across the board to divide the sky and the road.
4 To create a sense of movement, tear white and blue tissue paper into long strips. Invite the children to help you.
5 Using PVA glue and brushes, stick and overlap the tissue paper horizontally to fill the top section of the board.
6 Using poster paint mixed with sand, paint the lower section of the board with the children's help.
7 Look at an image of a 1950s London bus and create a simple outline design of a large, red London bus.
8 Copy the image onto the MDF board with a sketching pencil.
9 Paint the image of the bus using red poster paint with the children's help.
10 Use black poster paint for the wheels and details.
11 Invite the children to make 3D faces using tissue paper and wool.
12 Staple the faces to the windows of the bus.
13 Place a signpost showing the direction to Buckingham Palace on the display.

Wheels on the Bus

Create and use story cards with the children to emphasise the different stages of Alice and Nicholas's bus journey through London. Follow this by introducing the song *The Wheels on the Bus*, which will allow the children to bring the story to life through simple actions.

Resources

- The song *The Wheels on the Bus*
- Story photo cards (see page 17)

Approach

1. Make a set of A3 story photo cards (see page 17).
2. Sing the song *The Wheels on the Bus* and make up some simple actions for the children to perform.
3. Make up some extra verses for the song, using the story as an inspiration.
4. Ask the children to think of some words that describe the big, red bus as it trundles along on the way to Buckingham Palace.
5. Discuss with the children how they get to school every day. Do they travel by car, by bus or on foot?
6. Using the images on the photo cards, encourage the children to tell the story of *One and Two Halves to Buckingham Palace* in their own words.

A View from the Bridge

As the story *One and Two Halves to Buckingham Palace* is set in 1950s London, a tugboat full of coal on the River Thames would have been quite a familiar sight and one that is worthy of exploration in art. As Big Ben is such a famous landmark it would make a superb addition to the children's work and can be combined with a view of a tugboat passing by along the river.

The Tugboat and Big Ben

Resources

- Large MDF board
- White emulsion paint
- Cardboard boxes and tubes or cardboard
- Tissue paper in assorted colours
- PVA glue
- Cardboard
- Thick, white card
- Poster paint
- Paint brushes

Approach

1. Paint the board with white emulsion paint.
2. Tear blue, green and grey tissue paper into horizontal strips to create the water.
3. Using PVA glue, stick strips of tissue paper onto the board covering the background with overlapping colours to create the effect of the river.
4. Make a 3D tugboat from cardboard and paint it.
5. Paint some children on card, cut them out and place them in the tugboat.
6. Make a 3D Big Ben from cardboard and create texture with paint.
7. Add a white circular clock face to Big Ben.

London Bridge is Falling Down

Again, make and use a set of cards depicting the children's story illustrations to help children with sequencing the events in the story, this time focusing on the nursery rhyme *London Bridge is Falling Down*.

Resources

- A copy of *London Bridge is Falling Down*
- A complete set of photos of children's illustrations for each part of the story (this activity will need to be completed at the end of Creative Literacy Week)
- A4 paper

Approach

1 Ask the children to think of a name for their tugboat using alliteration, for example, Tony the Tugboat, then to write a short descriptive sentence.

2 Make a storyboard using photographs of all of the children's book illustrations and cut them out. Ask the children to work in groups of four to sequence the pictures and write a simple sentence underneath. Encourage the children to read their finished stories to the rest of the class.

3 Sing the song *London Bridge is Falling Down* with the children and add some simple actions for the children to perform.

Admiral Nelson and the Pigeons

In the 1950s Trafalgar Square was full of pigeons (today numbers are controlled to protect the statues and public health). An important part of a day out in London was a visit to Trafalgar Square to feed the pigeons. People could buy brown paper bags filled with birdseed to feed them. In the story *One and Two Halves to Buckingham Palace*, the pigeons have a prominent role to play and it is important to reflect this in the artwork. Nelson's column was a popular landmark in 1950s London and still is today.

Resources

- Life-size pigeon templates
- MDF board
- Pale blue emulsion paint
- Paint brushes
- Images of Admiral Nelson
- Poster paint
- Photocopies of pigeon feathers
- Scissors
- PVA glue
- Staple gun

Approach

1. Paint the background of the MDF board using pale blue emulsion paint.
2. Using images of Nelson as inspiration, paint a large picture of the admiral onto the board.
3. Invite the children to cut up the photocopied pigeon feathers and stick to the pigeon templates with glue.
4. Create a flock of pigeons by overlapping and bending the templates on the upper part of the display.

Book Blurb

Younger children often enjoy sharing their achievements with others and, with this in mind, encourage a group of older children to look at the children's work and write a blurb for the back cover of the book, focusing on the illustrations.

Resources

- Story photo cards (see page 17)
- A4 paper
- Pencils

Approach

1. Ask the children to write a different story opening for *One and Two Halves to Buckingham Palace* (or whichever story you have chosen).
2. Encourage the children to read their story openings aloud.
3. Discuss, with talking partners, ideas for a short magazine article about the story. Encourage the children to think of a catchy headline, for example, 'Boy's Head Stuck in Railings!' As a class, share ideas and write a short article about the incident.
4. Invite an older child to read the story openings, look at the illustrations and read the magazine article, and then to write a blurb for the back of the book. Ask them to share the blurb with the younger children.

Two of the guards marched smartly towards him and tried to pull him out but he would not budge! Spick and Span, two of the Queen's corgis, scuttled over and barked furiously at the hapless Nicholas but he still would not budge! The Queen, who heard all the commotion, ordered her footman to take a silver platter of cucumber sandwiches spread with thick, creamy butter over to Nicholas.

"This might do the trick," said the Queen with a twinkle in her eye.

The footman, smiling ruefully, spread the golden butter over Nicholas's ears but he still would not budge! Just then, a pigeon's feather drifted downwards and tickled his nose. ATISHOO! Nicholas sneezed loudly and his head popped out of the railings!

"Look Mummy, I am marching just like the soldiers!" he said gleefully.

Early next morning, a letter arrived special delivery! Inside was a grand invitation to take afternoon tea at Buckingham Palace. Their Royal Highnesses Princess Anne, Prince Charles and Spick and Span, the corgis, would be there too.

Can you guess what they had for tea?

5

A Visit to the Palace

The theme 'An Exciting Day Out' with London as the destination makes Buckingham Palace an ideal subject for a large class display. This grand historical building was just as popular in the 1950s as it is today. Encourage the children to capture its grandeur so it can be included as an eye-catching illustration to the story.

Resources

- MDF board
- Poster paints
- Brushes
- White emulsion paint
- Gold and black card
- Triangles of card
- Union Jack template
- Collage materials in red, white and blue
- Images of Buckingham Palace
- Felt pens
- Coloured pencils
- Scrap materials
- Ribbon or tape

Approach

1 Paint the MDF board with black emulsion paint.

2 Invite the children to paint the top of the board blue and add white clouds to create a sky.

3 Paint the shape of Buckingham Palace onto the board, adding detail in 2D and 3D.

4 Cut out vertical strips of gold and black card and attach them to the board to form railings. Leave the centre of the strips unattached.

5 To make bunting, give each child a card triangle and ask them to decorate it on one side with collage materials, using red, white and blue only.

6 Staple the triangles to a length of ribbon or tape, being careful to leave equal gaps between each triangle.

7 Weave the bunting in and out of the railings.

8 Invite a pair of children to colour in the Union Jack for the top of the building. Attach this to a straw and fix it in place.

9 Add finishing touches such as 3D characters, grass and flowers with pens, pencils, paint or collage materials and place on the display.

Performance Poetry

Bring the story to life by including some performance poetry. You could write your own poems or use famous examples from favourite poets and authors. 'Buckingham Palace' by AA Milne is an excellent piece to base recitals on. It could even provide the inspiration for a short song and dance to music. Writing your own poems, either as a class, or individually, is also an excellent way to inspire the children.

Resources

- The poem 'Buckingham Palace' by AA Milne
- The poem 'Visiting London' by Charlotte Parker (*Create and Display Interactive: Performing Arts*) or another poem of your choice
- A4 paper
- Colouring pencils

Approach

1 Set the poem 'Buckingham Palace' to music and sing with the children. Do some simple dance movements to go with the poem ready for a performance.

2 Read the poem 'Visiting London', or a poem of your choice, and make up some simple actions ready for performance.

3 Prepare the text for a simple invitation to take afternoon tea at Buckingham Palace.

4 Design your own party invitations and ask the children to decorate them with party things using repeating patterns. Leave spaces for children to fill in their names, the date, the time and the occasion.

A London Scene

A good way to convey how hectic and cosmopolitan a modern city can be is to choose a famous location that symbolises the hustle and bustle of a busy urban scene. The example on this page focuses on St Paul's Cathedral. London buses trundling along in the foreground help to create a lively atmosphere.

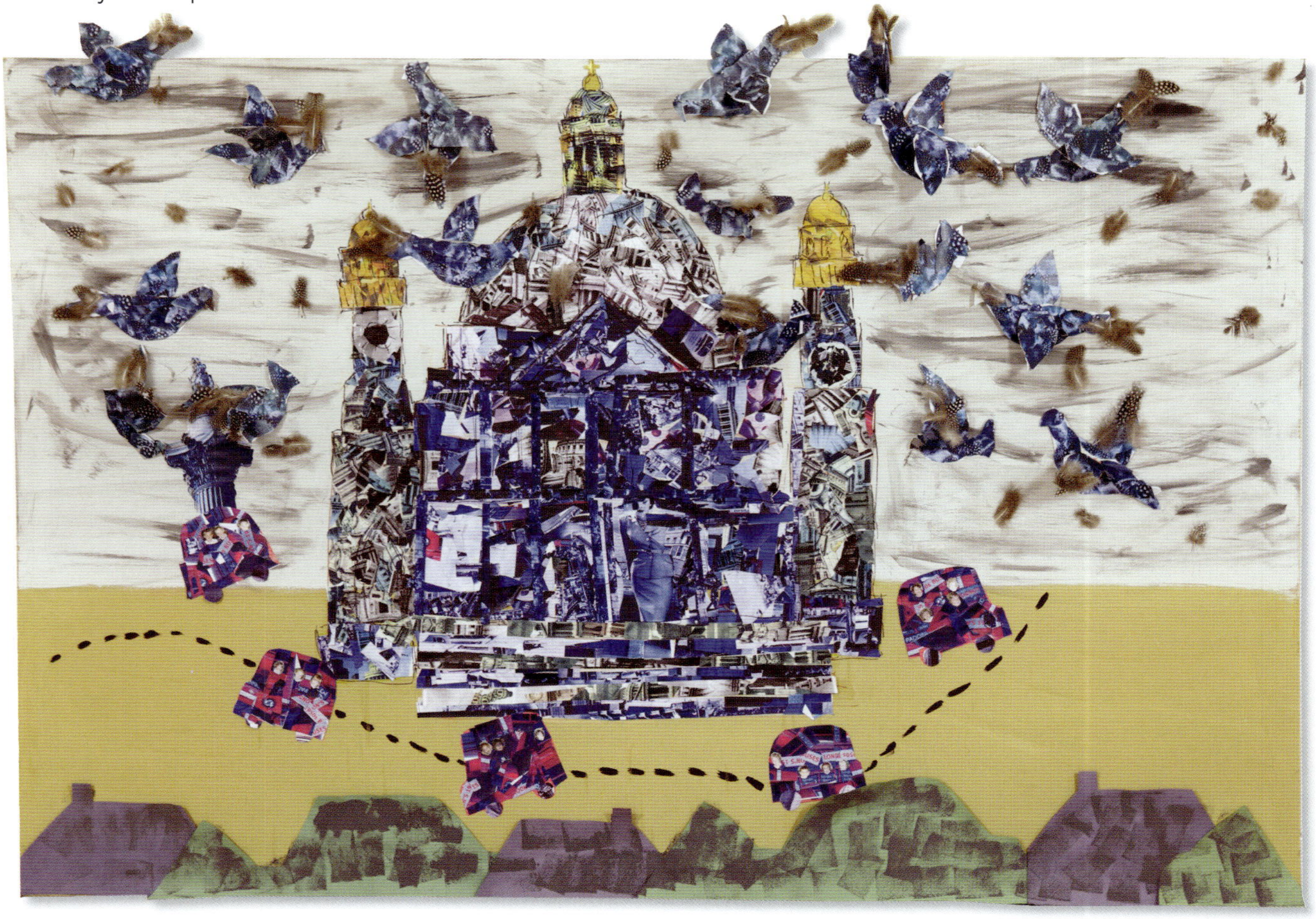

Resources

- Images of St Paul's Cathedral or another landmark building
- Collage materials including grey feathers
- Large MDF board
- Black emulsion paint
- Brushes
- Sketching pencil
- Poster paints
- Collage materials
- Glue
- Pigeon templates
- Thin card
- Black felt pens

Approach

1. Paint the background of the MDF board with black emulsion paint.
2. Draw an outline of a London landmark building such as St Paul's and its surroundings.
3. Paint the background and fill the building outline with collage materials.
4. Photocopy the pigeon templates onto thin card and give copies to the children.
5. Ask the children to paint the pigeon templates grey, and leave to dry.
6. Invite them to add texture and detail with black felt pens and collage materials.
7. Stick grey feathers onto the pigeons sparingly.
8. Starting from the top, fill the board with pigeons and pigeon wings, being careful to leave gaps.
9. Make some of the pigeons stand out from the display to create a 3D effect.
10. Complete the display by adding London buses to the foreground using collage materials.
11. You could create another scene depicting London Bridge using a similar approach.

A London Tea Party

Give the children the opportunity to write an alternative story ending to *One and Two Halves to Buckingham Palace*, or whichever story you are following. Encourage the children to read their story endings aloud and invite positive and constructive feedback from their audience.

Resources

- A4 paper
- Images of tea parties in the 1950s and today
- Story photo cards

Approach

1 Work with the children to design a menu for a tea party set in the 1950s. Illustrate the menu with fairy cakes, bowls of jelly and, of course, cucumber sandwiches. Discuss how a menu for a tea party today would be different from one in the 1950s.

2 Write a thank you letter from Alice and Nicholas to Prince Charles and Princess Anne for inviting them to afternoon tea.

3 Invite the children to write a different story ending for *One and Two Halves to Buckingham Palace.*

4 Encourage them to read their story endings aloud to the class and invite constructive feedback.

5 Ask a group of older children to read the story endings and write a review.

Example story endings:

1. "Servant," called the Queen, "get the children immediately." When the children arrived, Alice and Nicholas were a bit scared but Charles and Anne were not scared at all! The Queen smiled and presented each child a present. Charles got a book about soldiers and Anne got an art book, Nicholas got a new sailor suit and Alice a toy wooden horse. At that moment, Spick and Span barked and licked each of the children!

2. When they had tea the children played together. Soon after they were talking to Jewel, the Royal bunny. Meanwhile the Queen, Spick and Span were keeping an eye on them. Jewel loved visitors. When it was time to go home the children couldn't find their coats because Spick and Span had hidden them!

Final Performance

As a finale to Creative Literacy Week, ask each class to prepare a song, poem or simple dance routine that can be brought together in a collaborative performance. Each class could be given one of the themes in the story. Using your vibrant displays as a background set – along with dance, music, art and creative writing – will bring the story vividly to life.

Resources

- Large story displays as a background set to the performance
- Copies of *One and Two Halves to Buckingham Palace*, or your chosen story
- Copies of children's writing from the Creative Literacy Week
- Props linked to the story
- Photos of the children's story illustrations
- Projector and screen
- Music for singing and dance routines (some examples can be found in *Create and Display Interactive: Performing Arts*)

Approach

1 Create a vivid setting for a performance by putting the five large book illustrations on the stage as background props.

2 Display copies of the stories as well as the children's creative writing work.

3 Choose five children to be narrators with each child focusing on one illustration or theme.

4 Give the classes enough time to prepare and practise their performances. Try to include a range of different performances including performance poetry, dance, singing and mime.

5 Put on your show, ensuring that the narration includes cues for the different performances.

Illustrated Storybook

You can also use a story as a starting point for a variety of cross-curricular activities during Creative Literacy Week. As before, this example uses the story *One and Two Halves to Buckingham Palace*, but the ideas could be adapted to any suitable story. It is a good idea to encourage a collaborative approach, and one way would be to use the children's main displays as illustrations to enhance the text.

Resources

- Photos of the five main displays printed on A4 paper
- Copies of *One and Two Halves to Buckingham Palace*, or your chosen story
- A4 paper
- Book-making materials

Approach

1. Explain to the children that you are going to use their displays to make an illustrated storybook.
2. Make sets of cards depicting the five book illustrations. Arrange the text and images accordingly.
3. Invite a group of children to design and create a cover, and use the children's book blurbs to form a back cover. Use a book binder to hold the pages together.
4. Place a copy of the illustrated storybook in all of the classrooms so that children can choose to read it when appropriate.
5. Place a copy of the storybook in the library for others to read as a celebration of children's creativity.

Andy Warhol

Andy Warhol had an obsession with self-image that was portrayed frequently in his work. This project not only helps the children to discover how they are perceived by others but also gives ample opportunity for class discussion on friendship and the importance of individuality.

What's on your mind?

Resources

- Long rolls of paper (local printers will often give you roll ends for free)
- Sketching pencils and rubbers
- Watercolour pencils
- Felt pens

Approach

1 Position your class tables in two long rows and roll paper along the length. Alternatively, work on the floor. Arrange the children in two lines, facing each other over the paper.

2 Ask the children to spend some time observing the person opposite then to draw a general oval shape lightly with pencil on the part of the paper in front of them.

3 Ask them to draw a line horizontally through the centre of the oval and then vertically down the middle. Explain that this is roughly where the eyes and bridge of the nose should be.

4 Next, invite children to draw a small horizontal line halfway down the vertical line beneath the cross. This is where the mouth should be.

5 Now they should draw the classmate directly opposite them. The children should try to pick out features that they believe make this person an individual.

6 When they have drawn the features, start adding details with watercolour pencils and felt pens. Colours and shading can be used to give the portraits more expression.

7 Once everyone is happy with their friend's portrait, ask them to move to sit at the portrait of themselves, drawn by someone else.

8 Tell them that they must not change the facial features in the image but can make their portrait individual to them. Encourage them to use the space around their portrait's head to doodle their thoughts. They can use colour, diagrams, words and illustrations to express themselves. Doodling whatever is in their minds encourages a more expressive response to portraiture from children.

9 Hang the final drawing at the end of the session so that the children can appreciate how the class looks. Children might enjoy the challenge of identifying individuals just by scrutinising the doodles.

Pop Art

The Pop Artist Andy Warhol is an obvious starting point when asking a child to produce a self-portrait. His glossy silkscreen images transfer easily into basic computer-aided activities. By manipulating their own photographic images the children will find that they can individualise their portraits. The following activities will lead to a professional-looking pop art image with minimum effort.

Resources

- Examples of Andy Warhol portraits
- Computers with a basic graphics program (such as Fresco or Microsoft Paint)
- A clear digital portrait of each child
- Pencils
- A4 tracing paper
- 'Lick-and-stick' coloured paper
- Scissors
- A4 coloured card
- Glue sticks
- Poster paints
- Thin brushes

Approach

1 Look at Warhol's prints and discuss them in terms of what a print is, and why making a multiple image was important to the artist.

2 Using a basic graphics program, change the image to black and white. You may need to adjust the contrast for the desired effect.

3 Print out onto A4 paper.

4 Ask the children to place the tracing paper onto the black and white image and trace around the black shapes only.

5 Invite the children to dampen their 'lick-and-stick' paper, then to line up and attach the paper exactly over the tracing paper.

6 Ask them to carefully cut around the drawn shapes through both sheets of paper.

7 They can then position the 'lick-and-stick' paper shapes onto the coloured card and, when they are happy, stick them down with a glue stick.

8 As an extension activity, the children could also try painting the traced shapes with a limited pallet.

David Hockney

David Hockney (1937–) is an English painter and photographer. He is famous for his contribution to Pop Art, as well as being one of the most influential modern British artists.

Mirror Poems and Portraits

Choose a Hockney painting to use as a starting point for creative writing. The example used here is *Ann Putting on Lipstick* (1979). The artwork is a charcoal drawing of a woman wearing a long, spotted dress and high heels; she is peering into the mirror putting on her lipstick. The simplicity of the image makes it all the more striking; the essential moment when a woman applies the final touches of her make-up by applying her lipstick is captured perfectly. Discuss the image with children and then read the first four lines of Sylvia Plath's poem, 'Mirror'.

Mirror

I am silver and exact. I have no preconceptions.
Whatever I see I swallow immediately
Just as it is, unmisted by love or dislike.
I am not cruel, only truthful...

Sylvia Plath

Resources

- Image of the charcoal drawing *Ann Putting on Lipstick* by David Hockney
- A3 sketch paper
- Charcoal sticks
- Copy of Sylvia Plath's poem 'Mirror'
- A4 paper
- Pencils
- Mirrors
- Computers

Approach

1. Look at Hockney's drawing and discuss it in terms of composition, shape and mood.
2. Read the first four lines of Sylvia Plath's poem 'Mirror', and discuss it in terms of use of personification, choice of words and their effectiveness.
3. Display the charcoal drawing and ask the children to write their own four-lined poems, using Sylvia Plath's style as an inspiration. Encourage them to write the first draft in pencil and the final draft on the computer.
4. Working in twos, encourage one child to create a pose similar to the one in Hockney's drawing using a mirror as a prop. Ask the other child to do a quick sketch of the pose. They should then change places so that each child has a chance to hold a pose and do a sketch.
5. Using their first sketches along with the image of Hockney's painting as an inspiration, challenge the children to capture the simplicity of Hockney's style by doing their own quick sketches using only charcoal on A3 sketch paper.
6. Encourage the children to add something different to their portraits by altering some of the detail, for example, the style of shoes, the pattern in the dress or by adding an unusual hairstyle.
7. Display the poems with the charcoal portraits.
8. Arrange for the children to read their poems aloud to another class using their artwork and poetry display as a background.

I am flat yet possess unfathomable depths.
I hold no opinions.
I observe the world through my silver face,
As people watch themselves in me,
Reflected as they are, unblurred, unmarred.

I am plain and precise.
I make no pre-judgements.
Whatever I see, I return,
Identical, unchanged by feelings.
I am not a liar, but a reflection.

I am accurate and precise. I bear no love
or dislike.
Whatever appears to me
I will seize instantly.
Plain and clear, not letting feelings mask
the truth.
I am not brutal, but only pure.

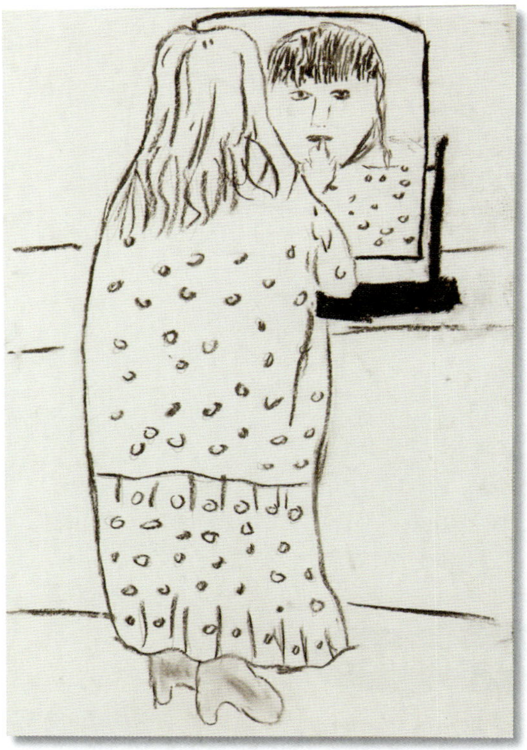

I am purposeful and decisive. I am unfazed by
sadness or grief.
Whatever I see, I digest sincerely
True to my word, unmisted by elation or
depression.
I am not biased, merely honest.

Continuous Line Portraits

Simplicity and clarity of form is evident in many of David Hockney's drawings. Using his work as a stimulus for a drawing activity can inspire children to have a more spontaneous approach to their own drawings. Permanent, continuous lines in ink encourage children to have a bold and confident style.

Approach

1. Ask the children to look at themselves in the mirror making different expressions.
2. Using a loaded brush and at the same time looking in the mirror, ask the children to follow the contours of their features while keeping their brush on their paper at all times.
3. Get the children to work with focus and encourage them to fill up the whole page before looking closely at their final piece.
4. Children can add details to their ink drawings at the end.

Approach

- A2 sketch paper
- Indian ink
- Soft brushes
- Mirrors

Abstract Ink and Tissue Paper Portraits

Encourage the children to focus on line and pattern in the continuous line drawings and then develop them into colourful, abstract images. They should focus on the most interesting area of their line drawings and then copy them onto collaged backgrounds. The final touch is achieved by using Indian ink to create a vibrant effect.

Resources

- Tissue paper in assorted colours
- Square pieces of card
- PVA glue and glue brushes
- Indian ink
- Soft brushes
- Sketching pencils

Approach

1. Ask the children to choose two or three different shades of tissue paper and tear them into pieces of varying sizes.
2. Ask them to fill the card with overlapping colours of tissue paper. They will need to stick the tissue paper down well and ensure that the surface is flat.
3. When the glue is dry, invite the children to choose a section from their continuous line portrait and copy it in pencil onto the collaged card.
4. Finally, they can go over the pencil lines with Indian ink.

René Magritte

René Magritte (1898–1967) was a Belgian surrealist artist. Through his paintings, he tried to challenge people's perceptions of reality and encourage them to be more aware of their surroundings.

Portrait of a Businessman

This activity uses René Magritte's painting *Son of Man* (1964) as inspiration for portraits containing symbols. Look at the painting and discuss the narrative behind the image. Who does the man represent? Does his appearance give us clues about who he is?

Approach

1. Discuss the routine involved in commuting to work every day, then ask the children to imagine a journey, thinking about the repetitive scenery they might encounter.
2. Using the images of businessmen, ask the children to select a figure, cut it out and stick it into their Ideas book. They should then sketch an imaginative setting around the figure.
3. Invite the children to transfer the outline of the chosen image onto A3 paper and redraw their setting, adding more detail if needed.
4. Encourage the children to add colour using Magritte's palette, working from the centre of the painting. (You may wish to look at other examples of Magritte's work such as *The Mysteries of the Horizon*, *The Human Condition* and *The Difficult Crossing*.)

Resources

- An image of Magritte's painting *Son of Man*
- Images of businessmen
- Ideas books
- Pencils
- Good quality A3 paper
- Brushes
- Acrylic paint
- Water pots
- Other examples of Magritte's work

The Bowler Hats

In René Magritte's painting *Son of Man* (1964) the figure is wearing a bowler hat. This image of the hat is used throughout many of Magritte's paintings and has become an iconic image. This activity requires the children to transform a basic bowler hat into a work of art.

Resources

- Bowler hats (from a theatrical costume shop)
- Scissors
- Glue gun
- Images of clocks and time pieces
- Card
- Acrylic paint
- Wire

Approach

1. Discuss well-known sayings about time, for example, 'time flies', 'running out of time', 'tick tock, tick tock' and so on.
2. Look at images of clocks and time pieces or invite the children to draw their own clock faces.
3. Using the clock images as inspiration, invite the children to create a time-related design for a bowler hat, then to construct their designs using the materials available.
4. Put the hats to one side, ready to use in the next stage of the project.

Stomp Performance

This activity gives older children the opportunity to create a dance routine linked closely to music and mime. Use a piece of artwork as inspiration for your routine, such as Magritte's painting *Son of Man*. The ideas suggested below are based on *Stomp*, which was chosen because of the way in which percussion and movement are linked to a storyline. As part of the 'Stomp' performance children need to understand how rhythm should be used in their performance. As part of the preparation for the piece, devise some simple musical exercises that can be taught by non-musicians; this approach has a profound effect on how the children understand rhythm and movement.

Preparation

Resources

- Basic percussion instruments

Approach

1 Stand in a circle with the children.
2 As the leader, create a simple rhythm using a combination of claps, clicks and stamps. Invite the children to echo your rhythm. As the exercise progresses, the rhythm patterns can become more complex, eventually including rests that can be represented by an added silent movement. Invite the children to take turns to be the leader if appropriate.
3 Say your name out loud and clap the rhythm, using the syllables in your name to create the beat (for example, Miss/us/Smith). Work around the circle, with the children saying their name and clapping the rhythm in turn.
4 Next, create a simple beat either by clapping or with a percussion instrument. Working around the circle, invite the children to clap and say their names to the rhythm, keeping in time with your beat. The children should try to stay in time but you can manipulate the rhythm where necessary, for example, by slowing down or becoming quieter.
5 Divide the class into small groups. Continue to clap an even beat and ask each group to perform their name rhythms together. This exercise creates a layering effect culminating in the whole class clapping their individual rhythms together. Percussion instruments can replace claps, clicks or stamps to enrich the timbre.

A Robotic Dance

The 'Stomp' performance in this example revolved around a train journey with robotic commuters. As a contrast, some more relaxed drummers provided the music. The final performance could involve the children performing to an audience in costume, using music, mime and dance to create an amusing and engaging piece of work. Use the decorated bowler hats that the children made in the previous activities and some plain white masks to enhance the idea of commuters all acting the same and to emphasise the robotic feel of the piece.

Resources

- Drums and drum sticks
- Boom whackers
- Decorated bowler hats
- White masks
- Chairs for the train
- Newspapers

Approach

1 Explain to the children that a constant pulse or beat is a crucial part of *Stomp*.
2 In a circle, ask the children to move to different beats in a bar, for instance, stepping on just beat 1, then stepping on beats 1 and 3, and so on.
3 On the silent beats children need to freeze so that their movements have a robotic element.
4 During the dance activity, ask some children to play percussion instruments and also to create rhythms by playing drumsticks on the floor, wall or on the chair legs. A conductor's whistle could mark the start of the dance.
5 For the performance, the children should wear their bowler hats and white masks to create just the right atmosphere. They could be seated as if on a train and hold newspapers to enhance the feel of uniformity.

Imaginative Settings

Drawing is a fundamental element of art. It is simple and available to everyone. By altering children's perceptions of what it means to make a good drawing, children will gain confidence in their own visual language. It is often tempting to follow the path well-trodden in promoting drawing at school. The activity is usually observational or formulaic. These drawing strategies have their place but it is often through less structured lessons that a child's true creativity is channelled. The following examples are starting points for class work on the theme of environment. Using storytelling as inspiration, the children use their imaginations to express their reaction to a setting created by the teacher. In turn this work can lead to discussion about issues raised or simply act as a visual guide for the child's re-telling of the story.

Mind's Eye Drawings

Resources

- A large space such as the hall
- Tranquil music
- Large sheets of paper
- A copy of the poem 'The Lake Isle of Innisfree' by WB Yeats (available online) or a story or poem of your choice
- Chalks, felt pens and crayons

Approach

1 Create a calm atmosphere to the start of the lesson by dimming lights and playing tranquil music as the children are seated on the floor.

2 Place a large sheet of paper in front of each child, making sure they have enough space to work comfortably.

3 Ask the children to remain quiet and explain that they are going to create a drawing entirely from their imagination. Tell them that their imagination is going to help them to see a story in their 'mind's eye'. This is a good phrase to use as children tend to relate this concept to daydreaming. The phrase 'daydreaming' will also reinforce the importance of imagination.

4 With the music still quietly playing in the background, ask the children to close their eyes and begin to recite your story or poem.

5 When you have finished reading, ask the children to open their eyes. Ask some leading questions about what picture they saw in their mind's eye as you spoke. Concentrate on visual or sensory aspects of the text, for example, what time of day they thought it was or what the weather was like.

6 Tell the children that you are going to read the text again but this time you would like them to concentrate on the part of the story or poem that gave them the strongest picture, and to draw this as you read. Explain that you want them to fill their sheets of paper with their ideas, using drawing tools of their choice. Emphasise that the drawings don't have to be perfect. The most important thing is that their drawings show the feelings they have when they hear the words.

7 Give each child a free choice of drawing tools such as chalks, felt pens and wax crayons. Limit the colours to three of four shades.

8 Before reading again, make sure the music is still playing, and remind the children to concentrate on their drawing only. Read the text two or three times, pausing between sections. Some children will naturally love the freedom this activity promotes but others will be intimidated at first. Make sure you encourage all participants, however challenging they find the activity.

9 When you have finished reading, let the children finish what they have been drawing and then pick two examples from the class. Reiterate that each drawing will be an individual response to the story and that there is no right or wrong way of expressing themselves.

Collaborative Weather Drawings

Creative drawing activities should have exciting and varied starting points for young children. It is important that, as teachers, we explore different approaches and means of expression with our classes so that children's visual confidence grows. Interpreting a drawing and exploring how forms can change as the image develops has been a method used by artists for centuries. Often this exploration of the surface of the paper and drawing tool is instinctive. The following activity offers an alternative way of allowing children to experience how a drawing can develop without becoming self-conscious or inhibited by their skills.

Approach

1 Before the lesson, mentally prepare to tell the children about an experience, real or imaginary, where you have encountered dramatic weather.
2 Ask the children to sit in a large circle on the floor. Create a calm atmosphere by dimming the lights.
3 Place a large sheet of paper in front of each child, making sure they have enough space to work comfortably.
4 Ask the children to remain quiet and explain that they are going to create a drawing coming entirely from their imagination.

Resources

- Charcoal
- A large space such as the hall
- Large sheets of paper
- Coloured chalk
- Music that suggests dramatic weather conditions such as Vivaldi's *Four Seasons*
- Wall space to display the work
- Sticky tack

going to improve this drawing by adding weather. At this point start the music you have chosen. Encourage the children to use the whole page and to work quickly without spoiling the previous drawing.

10 Continue this pattern around the circle, giving children no more than three minutes to work on each piece of art. The children should gain confidence during this activity as the process of working on so many drawings helps them to become less anxious about producing a finished piece.

11 Enlist the children in helping to place all of their drawings together in a suitable place as a large display. View them as a group and explain that every drawing is a shared drawing. Which one has worked best and why?

5 Invite the children to share any stories of a time they have been in dramatic weather. Perhaps they got caught in heavy rain, snow or wind? How did they feel? What did they see? What sound could they hear? What happened to the light?

6 Tell them your dramatic weather story, being sure to include a distinctive setting. Perhaps you are on the top of a mountain or on a boat?

7 When you have finished telling your story, hand out the chalks. Ask the children to start their picture by drawing a line across the page. This can be wavy or straight and will form the horizon.

8 Ask the children to put down the chalk and sensibly move to the drawing of the person on their left. Ask them to look at the line drawn and add some other landmarks such as trees or buildings, depending on the setting of your story.

9 Follow the previous procedure by moving again to the left so that each child is looking at a new drawing. Tell them they are

Viewpoints

As a starting point for this project we chose a suitable piece of artwork with an environmental setting – the painting *An Autumn Landscape with a View of Het Steen in the Early Morning* by Peter Paul Rubens (1636). This expansive landscape shows a view of the stone house that was the artist's home. The painting is full of clues about the time of day and the season it depicts. The colour of the countryside foliage and the flowering plants in the foreground indicate an autumn scene. You can choose any image containing a home within an evocative landscape as the focus. Google Earth® is an excellent resource for this activity.

Pastel Landscapes

Resources

- A copy of Rubens' painting *An Autumn Landscape with a View of Het Steen in the Early Morning*, or an image of your choice
- Soft pastels
- Coloured A3 sugar paper
- Rubbers
- Google Earth®

Approach

1 Focus on the sky in the painting and encourage the children to imagine they are looking down on Rubens' landscape.

2 Encourage the children to see their aerial view as a patchwork of patterns.

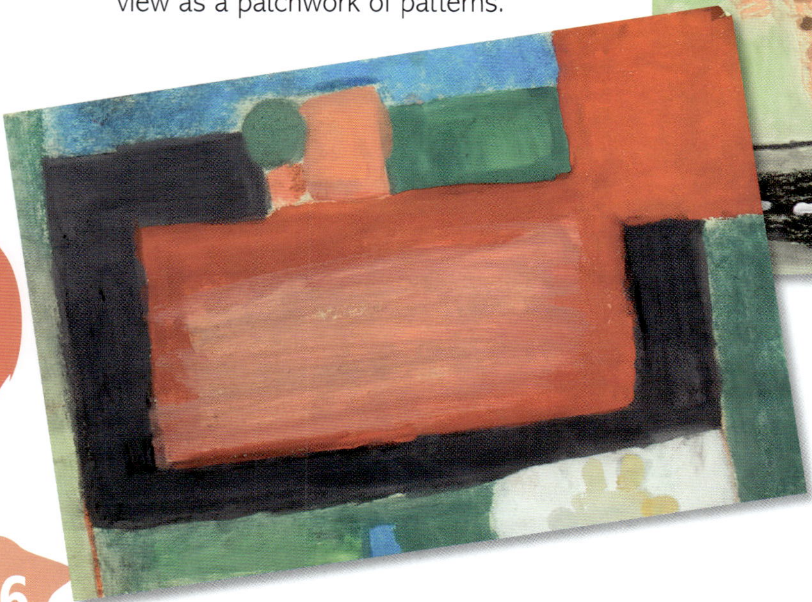

3 Using soft pastels, ask the children to fill their page with shapes that explain the landscape. They should focus on texture and colour.

Mixed-media Patchwork

Looking at An Autumn Landscape with a View of Het Steen in the Early Morning by Peter Paul Rubens (1636), use the composition, colours and textures as an inspiration for making a patchwork wall hanging. Take care to choose art materials that reflect the hues in the painting. You could use a different work of art linked to your current themes.

Resources

- *An Autumn Landscape with a View of Het Steen in the Early Morning* by Peter Paul Rubens (1636) or an image of your choice
- Pastel paintings from the previous activity
- Canvas squares (of equal size)
- Sketching pencils
- Acrylic paints
- Paper plates for mixing colours
- Paint brushes
- Sequins, beads, scraps of fabric and other collage materials
- Glue brushes and glue
- Needles and a selection of threads
- Glitter glue
- Sewing machine

Approach

1. Look again at the painting *An Autumn Landscape with a View of Het Steen in the Early Morning* by Rubens or your chosen image, focusing on the colours.
2. Ask the children to copy the basic shapes from their landscape painting onto the canvas squares using a pencil.
3. Invite the children to mix the paints on the paper plates to reflect the colours in the painting and then to paint the background on the canvas squares. Leave to dry.
4. The children can then embellish the canvas squares with collage materials to create texture and detail. Encourage them to use a variety of sewing, sticking and beading techniques to create a vibrant collage.
5. Stitch the canvas squares together with a sewing machine to create the final patchwork wall hanging.

Unusual Viewpoints

This project uses a science lesson as a starting point for creating vibrant images reflecting what children see when looking down a microscope.

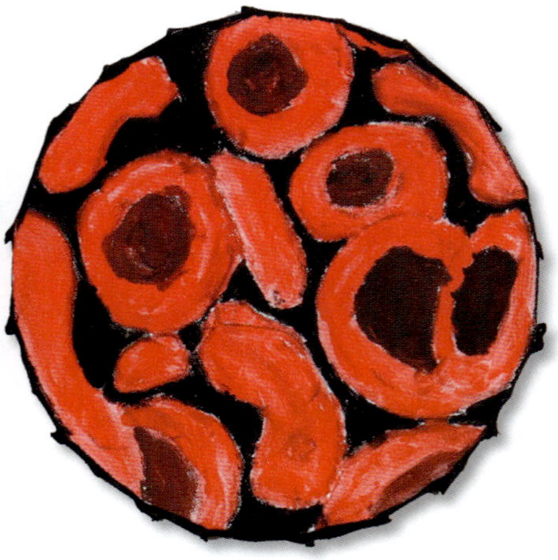

Resources

- Images of stained cells
- Circular canvases
- Sketching pencils
- Oil paints
- Brushes
- Microscope

Approach

1 Encourage the children to look at pictures of stained cells under the microscope. Looking through the microscope gives them a circular field of vision; this will help them to create a round image.

2 Ask the children to sketch the outline of cells onto the circular canvas.

3 They can then add paint, to re-create the images as seen under the microscope.

4 Place the circular paintings together to make a vibrant display.

Ideal Homes

This activity focuses on the importance of using emotive language and eye-catching design as part of the creative process involved in producing an advertisement. Encourage the children to think imaginatively about the sort of fantasy home they would like to live in and design an advertisement to promote it.

Resources

- Estate agents' brochures or websites for country estates or castles
- Ideas books
- A2 cartridge paper
- Sketching pencils
- Felt pens
- Rulers

Approach

1 Using the property details of the country estates and castles, discuss what children's ideal homes would include. Focus on setting, facilities and design. Ask the children to make visual notes in their Ideas books.

2 Draw a border the width of a ruler on the edge of the A2 sheet. Then divide the space inside the border into any four shapes.

3 Ask the children to draw a bird's eye view plan of their ideal home in one of the shapes.

4 In the second shape, they should draw the house in its setting from a distance.

5 In the third shape, ask them to draw the front elevation of their property.

6 The fourth shape should feature a drawing of an interior view of a room.

7 Invite the children to add colour with pencils, pens or both.

8 Discuss with the children the importance of using persuasive language to capture the reader's attention. As a class, list some examples of emotive words that could be placed as key words on their advertisements to make them even more eye-catching.

9 Ask the children to think of a logo for their advertisements and invite volunteers to give a presentation to the rest of the class about the final pieces. Encourage the children to comment on their own work and the work of others.

The Sea

The artist JMW Turner (1775–1851) is famous for his watercolour landscapes portraying weather and atmosphere. Turner was one of the first artists to create his paintings in the outdoor environment and this had a profound effect on his compositions and techniques. The aim of this short art project is to encourage the children to work with spontaneity and increase their visual confidence.

Watercolour Seascapes

Resources

- Examples of Turner's watercolour paintings such as *Shipwreck of the Minotaur* and *Calais Pier*
- Watercolour palettes or tubes
- Watercolour paper
- Soft brushes
- Water
- Pots

Approach

1. Focus on the atmosphere created by Turner's seascape paintings. Ask the children to imagine what it would feel like to be in the paintings.
2. Share experiences of extreme weather situations focusing on children's emotional responses.
3. Using brushes dipped in water, ask the children to drench the watercolour paper and quickly paint a horizontal line to define the horizon.
4. At this stage, they should use a wet-on-wet technique causing paint to bleed and create a watery seascape.
5. Ask the children to paint horizontal lines across the paper using Turner's colour palette. Tell them that they will need to work quickly for the best effect.
6. Encourage them to give the seascape more depth by using stronger tones in the foreground with lighter ones in the background.
7. Children may want to add detail into their work. If they do, encourage them to use purples to enhance a sense of space.

Seashore Mobiles

The aim of this project is to create abstract mobiles based on the textures and colours of the sea. Gather a collection of objects found on the seashore and create a texture table based on a seaside theme. Encourage children to handle the objects and use descriptive words to explain their different textures and colours.

Resources

- Thick white card cut into even shapes
- A collection of objects from the seashore such as shells, pebbles, driftwood and feathers
- Bradawl (to be used under supervision)
- Glitter, sawdust, cotton wool, feathers and tissue paper
- Powder and poster paints
- Sponges
- Ideas books
- Sticky tack
- Fishing wire

Approach

1. Give each child three white card shapes.
2. Demonstrate the different materials, colours and techniques that can be used to create texture.
3. Ask the children to experiment with some of the various techniques to create texture in their Ideas books.
4. Invite them to decorate both sides of their shapes using contrasting textures and colours.
5. Ask the children how they would like to arrange their shapes.
6. Under very close adult supervision, let the children make holes at the top of the shape by pushing the bradawl very carefully through the card into the sticky tack.
7. Thread the shapes together with fishing wire and hang them up to create a display of colour and texture.
8. Coloured lights could be projected onto the images to enhance the display.

Mousehole Cat Illustrations

Use the story *The Mousehole Cat* by Antonia Barber (Walker Books, 1993) as a starting point for creating colourful illustrations to go with the story. Read *The Mousehole Cat* to the children without showing the illustrations and then talk about the images evoked by the story. Encourage the children to share their ideas and then give each child an extract from the text to illustrate.

Resources

- *The Mousehole Cat* by Antonia Barber
- Images of cats
- Ideas books
- Pencils
- Wax crayons
- Water-based paints
- Brushes
- Paint palettes
- A3 cartridge paper

Approach

1 Invite the children to try out some ideas for illustrations in their Ideas books, including drawing a cat.
2 Demonstrate and let children practise the wax resist technique. Wax resist is a technique where wax crayon is used on paper and then water-based paint is applied over the top to create contrasting textures.
3 Get each child to look closely at a part of the story from *The Mousehole Cat* and ask them to sketch out their compositions in their Ideas books.
4 When they are happy with their work, they can transfer it to A3 paper. Remind them to draw in the outlines and details with wax crayons and use the paints to finish the picture.
5 Display the children's illustrations with the extracts from the book.
6 Encourage the children to discuss their own work and the work of others and to compare their illustrations with the original ones.
7 Give children the opportunity to present their work to a younger class by telling the story in their own words and using their illustrations as a storyboard.

Fantasy Fish

Look at Paul Klee's paintings *The Golden Fish,* (1925) or *Fish Magic,* (1925) and discuss them in terms of colour, shape and composition. Look for a biological diagram of a fish and talk to the class about the different parts, concentrating on colour and texture.

Resources

- A copy of *The Golden Fish* or *Fish Magic* by Paul Klee
- A biological diagram of a fish
- Ideas books
- Pencils, crayons and felt pens
- Rainbow-coloured scraperboards and sticks
- Fish shapes cut out of A4 coloured card
- A4 black card
- Tissue paper and crêpe paper
- Ribbon, pipe cleaners, sequins and jewels
- Acrylic shapes

Resources

1 After looking at the Klee painting and drawings of fish, ask the children to practise drawing fish in their Ideas books.

2 They should try out different colours and include some fantasy fish shapes.

3 Give each child a scraperboard and ask them to use this to continue the design process, using the stick to draw an outline and add patterns. The scraperboards could be stuck into the Ideas books.

4 Invite the children to choose a paper fish shape and stick it onto black card.

5 Encourage them to use the collage materials to give the fish a 3D effect.

6 Mount the fantasy fish onto a coloured background to create an eye-catching display.

Urban Art – Banksy

Banksy's work appears in the urban environment as if by magic. Even though his work has become synonymous with Street Art, the artist remains unknown although there has been much speculation as to his identity. For Banksy, the positioning of his stencils on the street is as important as the subject itself. He uses recycled images and text to convey a powerful message and he cleverly uses the urban environment to make comment on everyday life. Children respond enthusiastically to his use of humour and the way he takes one image and turns it on its head.

Selecting an Image

Resources

- Appropriate stencilled images by Banksy
- Access to the internet
- A simple graphics program such as Fresco or Microsoft Paint®
- A3 paper

Approach

1 Look at some appropriate stencilled images by Banksy and discuss with the children the effectiveness of his work.

2 Explain that they are going to create their own Banksy-style stencils using the same process as the artist.

3 Choose a theme for the children to research, for example, people at work, animals or popular culture. Ask them to use the internet to find an image that appeals to them. Explain that bold, simple images with contrasting tones are likely to work best.

4 Encourage them to think about where the image could appear in the school environment.

5 Ask the children to copy and paste their chosen image into the graphics program and to change it to just black and white.

6 Print the image as large as possible onto A3 paper.

Stencils and Sprays

Banksy leaves his stencils on a variety of surfaces and it is important to use the correct type of spray or paint depending on the age group of the children and on the surface you are working on. The same applies to the sort of cutting implements used, as craft knives are preferable but not safe or practical for younger children. The beauty of the stencil is that once it is made it can be used to embellish everyday environments.

Resources

- A3 printed images (previous activity)
- A3 thin card
- Spray mount
- Scissors or craft knives (teacher to supervise)
- Cutting board
- Masking tape
- A2 cartridge paper
- Enamel or textile spray in black, shades of grey and white
- Black, white and grey poster paint and sponges (for younger children)

Approach

1 Stick the A3 printed images onto the thin card using spray mount, being careful to keep it smooth.

2 Invite the children to carefully cut out the whole outline of the image, leaving the shape intact. This can be done by making a neat cut from the side and then taping the cut back together later. Keep both pieces!

3 Using the cut-out piece, ask the children to select the areas that will become shadow and cut these out. This process can be repeated depending on the detail wanted on the final image. Keep all of the pieces!

4 Demonstrate to the children how the stencilling should be done. Using cartridge paper as a base, select the first outline image (the first piece cut out from the centre) and spray mount onto base paper. Spray with the black colour evenly and let it dry.

5 Peel off the stencil to reveal the shape.

6 Continue this process, placing each consecutive cut-out piece over the image and spraying with a lighter shade, ending with white.

7 Invite the children to take turns at stencilling, under supervision. Younger children could use poster paints and stencils instead of the spray.

8 Look at the way Banksy uses text to enhance his work and get the children to create their own statements which link with their work and to write these on their artwork. The children could also add colour and drawings to the images, using Banksy's work as inspiration.

9 As a final touch, ask the children to think of using a pseudonym that they can use to sign off their work in the style of Banksy.

Urban Dance Project

Continuing with the theme of Urban Art, create a 'street' scene in which to carry out an urban-style dance.

Preparation

Resources

- Children's stencil pictures from the previous activity
- Suitable 'street' props such as old newspapers, rubbish bins, signs
- Baseball caps
- Baggy tops/hoodies and colourful t-shirts
- Tracksuit bottoms
- Suitable urban dance music (such as the examples provided on *Create and Display Interactive: Performing Arts*)

Approach

1 Use the stencil images created by the children as a backdrop for a dance performance.
2 Select suitable props and other items to improve the scene, such as old newspapers, rubbish bins, or street signs (made with the class). You could even create a mock-up lamp post if practical.
3 Ask the children to bring in and wear baggy, colourful t-shirts, tracksuit bottoms and baseball caps turned backwards or to the side.
4 Children should perform in bare feet, rather than trainers, so as to have more control over their movements.

Performance

Together with your class, devise a dance style that is street/urban – you could combine it with a different contemporary style for variety, for example, by giving it a Latin American twist. As street dance is so popular, this is a good way to get boys enjoying dance.

5 Listen to the music in small sections and work on one section at a time.

6 For section one, you could divide the class into three rows with starting positions. Assign each row a simple bold, repetitive move. When they are put together, they will look more complicated. For section two, the rows could move as one.

7 Continue to choreograph different moves for each section. Concentrate on one section in each session so that it is not overwhelming.

8 During rehearsals some children could be asked to choreograph their own sections in the middle.

9 Perform the urban dance routine using the Banksy-inspired images as a backdrop.

Urban Art – Keith Haring

Keith Haring was an artist who used the urban environment of New York to create vibrant stylised murals. Some of his images have a child-like quality and as a result are very accessible to children. In this project there are two clear stages – a drawing activity leading to a final painting.

Monster Doodles

Resources

- Images of Keith Haring's work
- Ideas books
- Sketching pencils
- Rubbers
- A3 coloured card
- Black felt pens

Approach

1 Focus on some of Keith Haring's large-scale paintings and discuss his use of bold, simple designs.

2 Working in their Ideas books, ask the children to take their pencils for a walk on the page to form round, smooth shapes.

3 Encourage the children to look at the shapes they have formed. Tell them that their monster doodle will take shape when they add eyes, arms, legs, teeth, scales and any other monster features. Invite them to do this.

4 Ask the children to start work on the A3 coloured card in pen by drawing a larger doodle and adding monster features. By using a pen, it forces the children to adapt their mistakes rather than erase them.

5 Mount the work in groups choosing different coloured backgrounds to emphasise their vibrancy.

Street Art Paintings

In his paintings Keith Haring uses strong colours and bold images to create exciting compositions. Encourage the children to use their monster doodles as inspiration for making large canvases. The aim is to show children how paintings can be created by using layers of colour and pattern.

Resources

- The children's monster doodles
- 10cm square 'viewfinders' (see below)
- Scissors
- Ruler
- Thin card
- Modelling clay
- Square canvas
- Sketching pencils
- Rubbers
- Acrylic paint
- Paint brushes
- Water pots

Approach

1 Make viewfinders from thin card. To do this, draw a square with a ruler and pencil on the card then place a ball of modelling clay under the card. Using scissors, push them firmly into the modelling clay to make a hole safely. Cut out the square window.

2 Ask the children to select a section of their monster doodle and place a viewfinder over it to frame the area.

3 Copy the area in the viewfinder onto the canvas using light pencil strokes, remembering that the corners of the canvas represent the corners of the viewfinder window. Rubbers

can be used on the canvas, if necessary.

4 Ask the children to limit their choice of paint to four colours – two pale and two strong.

5 They should begin by painting the whole canvas with the pale colours, alternating the colours for each section. Leave to dry.

6 Using the image seen through the viewfinder, they can then concentrate on adding more of the details seen in the pattern with pencil.

7 Working with the two strong coloured paints, invite the children to add more colour by following the pencil outlines over the pale sections. They should leave some of the pale sections exposed. Leave to dry.

8 Discuss the effect of the colours and encourage the children to add more layers using additional colours. Make sure each layer is completely dry before adding the next layer.

9 Using a thin brush, outline the shapes and add extra detail in black. Encourage the children to vary the thickness of the lines to give a spontaneous effect.

The School Play

The school play has become an integral and exciting part of the creative curriculum in many schools. During drama sessions linked to a performance, children should be given the opportunity to develop the skills necessary to communicate dramatic text to an audience. This experience is a hugely rewarding one, where children learn the importance of teamwork, being organised and ultimately having fun! It is possible to get children or teachers to write their own playscript collaboratively, perhaps using a story as an inspiration; the other option is to use a published play that often includes a script, score and CD. This chapter used a published playscript, *What a Knight!* by Craig Hawes (Musicline Publications, 2009) that has catchy melodies and elements of comedy. A good policy is to give every child who would like to be in the school play the opportunity to take part. Sometimes you can have more children than there are parts to play and, in this situation, it is always possible to either divide up the parts or to create additional lines to include some contemporary humour. It is important that each person in the cast is given a speaking part so that everyone feels a real sense of contribution.

Casting and Auditions

Approach

1 At auditions give a description of the characters to the prospective cast and then read through the script. Stop reading to explain jokes, demonstrate timing and play around with character voices.

2 Decide on different parts for the cast and tell them what their parts are going to be. Give the children their own scripts.

3 Ask the children to design an illustrated programme for the performance that can be handed out to the audience as they arrive. As part of the programme, include a synopsis of the story with some images taken during rehearsals.

Rehearsals

As part of preparing for a school play, children need to be given the opportunity to develop skills for effective oral communication of the written word. Such an experience equips them to present ideas impressively and expressively, and increases their confidence through performance.

Approach

1. Encourage the children to makes notes on their scripts and to highlight their lines so that they are clear about when they are speaking.
2. Focus on rehearsing a scene a week to begin with and decide where characters will enter and exit before the rehearsal.
3. Rehearse the songs with all the cast involved a couple of times a week.
4. Arrange the cast into different groups during the singing and add simple gestures during songs to create a more lively performance.
5. Encourage the children not just to act when they are speaking but also to react when they are not speaking.
6. Let the children experiment with movement and expression during rehearsals.
7. Half way through rehearsals, rehearse two or three scenes together so that the cast can see how they run on from each other.
8. In the last third of the rehearsals, ask the cast to learn their lines so that they get used to not using a script.
9. The stage crew do not need to attend rehearsals until nearer performance time.

Set, Sound and Lighting

It is a good idea to think about props, set design, sound and lighting in the early stages of planning for a school play. The set design needs to be simple but effective; the props need to be robust, as children tend to be quite heavy-handed with them. Using microphones for children who have singing parts and for those who have quiet speaking voices makes a dramatic improvement to the final performance. The sound and the lighting add to the overall effect and need to be thought through carefully to create the right atmosphere.

Approach

1 Create the set with a few wooden frames with fabric stretched over them. Use staples to attach the fabric to the frame. This type of frame is called a flat.
2 Paint the background of the frames with fabric paint and then add more detail as required.
3 Props need to be resourced quite early on so that they can be rehearsed with.
4 Each time characters exit the stage, their microphones should be switched off so that off-stage talking doesn't distract from the action on the stage.
5 Lighting projected onto the flats enhances the scenery and can be very effective. Use bright, happy colours such as oranges and yellows for the good characters.
6 Use blues and greens for the bad characters. These colours are also effective for giving the scenery a creepy feel.
7 The lighting usually changes during the songs to help create the right atmosphere.
8 The set will need to be constructed, costumes hung up and props laid out during the last week before the performance. Tables on wheels are useful if children are going to be the stage hands.

Costumes

A script can be brought to life by providing the audience with an evening of spectacular colour, with an emphasis on vibrant costumes, which can be either bought or made. Encouraging parents to assist can help when purchasing things like hats, tiaras or other small items. However, if there is time, creating your own costumes can be effective and rewarding!

Approach

1 Costumes need to be resourced quite early on so that they can be adjusted. Have a practice run with make-up and costumes and use the opportunity to have photographs taken of the cast and set. (But don't let the children wear the costumes for rehearsing until the dress rehearsal, as they need to be kept in good condition.)
2 Ask the children to bring in a named bag and coat hanger then, as their costumes are collated over the weeks, they can be kept together.
3 Make sure that the cast get a chance to have a dress rehearsal, with feedback given at the end of the session.
4 Invite a small audience to the dress rehearsal to give children a feel for how it will be. You are then ready for the final performance!

Make-up and Creating Characters

Make-up is an important part of any school play. Children will gain the most from the experience if you organise a realistic make-up and wardrobe department, where they can go and get into costume, and go through the make-up process. This might be a good opportunity to get additional help from parents and teaching assistants as a large number of children will need to be made up in a short period of time!

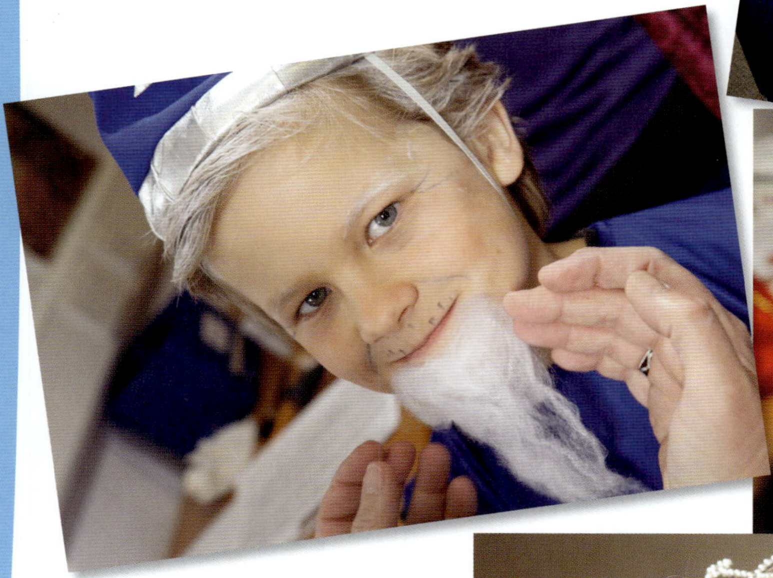

Resources

- A selection of make-up
- Brushes
- Clips and ribbons
- Mirrors and chairs

Approach

1 Delegate a specific room near the site of the performance dedicated to make-up – it is easier if it is close to boys' and girls' changing rooms so that the children can get dressed then enter make-up.

2 Make sure that you have plenty of time for preparing make-up.

3 Enlist make-up and wardrobe assistants to help you.

4 Some children will need to have their hair prepared ready for the performance.

5 Have props, accessories, and other items of clothing to hand to perfect their characters on the big night.

Performance Night

The big night of the school play can be a daunting experience, but handled well can also be fun and rewarding. As performers on the stage, children take an enormous step up the confidence ladder by understanding how to communicate to so many people expressively and audibly. Getting to grips with their nerves and the need to work as part of a team are also invaluable skills for life. Working together as a team on a school play definitely gives children the confidence to try their hand at other exciting ventures in the future! Such an experience will enable them not to fear moments, in their future lives, where they will have to speak in public.

Resources

- Photographs of the performance
- Reviews of the performance
- Quotes from the audience

Approach

1 For the final performance, the set will be constructed, costumes hung up and props laid out.
2 Children will need to be alert and ready to take their cues at the right time. The key is to be prepared, be organised and have fun!
3 After the performance, put a selection of photographs on display to celebrate the children's success.

4 Include photographs and reviews of the performance in a school newsletter or school magazine.
5 Gather quotes from the audience after the performance and display with the photographs.
6 Ask the children to write a review of the performance including a quote from a member of the audience. Comment on costumes, choreography, props, lighting and singing. Focus on using an eye-catching heading and a powerful opening paragraph to engage the reader's interest. Display the reviews with photographs of the performance.

A School Magazine

A perfect way to celebrate children's creative achievements is to produce a school magazine where the main focus is on the Creative Arts. A school magazine offers an ideal opportunity to showcase children's work in the Performing Arts and serves as a permanent reminder of all the exciting and innovative projects that are an important part of the creative curriculum. Working with an editorial team, with a teacher as editor and children as members of the team, can be hugely successful. Using a collaborative approach enhances children's confidence as well as being great fun.

Resources

- A range of artwork from children's work in the Creative Arts
- Ideas books
- Photographs of art, drama and music lessons

Approach

1 Ask the children to look at a range of artwork and photographs taken from work in the Creative Arts.
2 Working together, choose a selection of photographs and artwork that can be used in the school magazine.
3 Look at the children's Ideas books and choose a selection of work for the magazine.
4 Choose a powerful image for the front cover, for example, a strong photograph from the final performance of the school play.

A Useful Resource

A school magazine is a wonderful resource that can be used effectively in many lessons; it inspires a range of valuable activities closely linked to the Creative Arts, with an emphasis on flexible and collaborative learning. Children are always delighted to see their work in print, and planning a magazine gives them an ideal opportunity to discuss their work and the work of others. A school magazine will also reflect the variety and quality of children's work linked to the Creative Arts.

Resources

- A selection of magazine articles or school magazines
- Notebooks
- Examples of children's work
- Pencils

Approach

1 Look through a selection of magazine articles with the children and ask them to comment on effective headings and opening lines.
2 Focus on articles linked to the Creative Arts and ask the children to make notes on articles and images that they find engaging.
3 Discuss the importance of creating a layout that is image rich and eye catching.

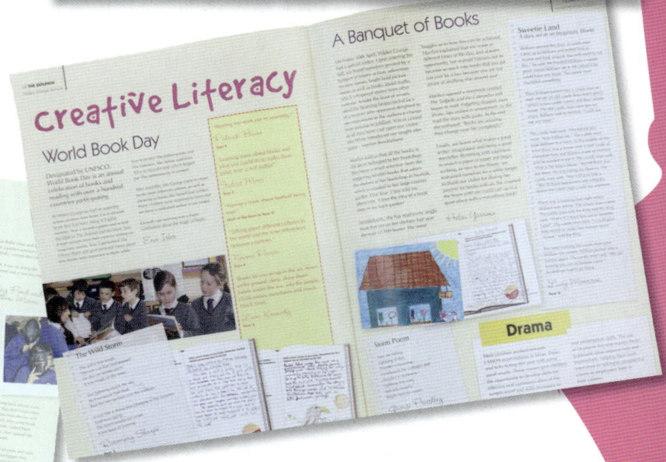

The Editorial Team

In any magazine the editorial team play a crucial role in organising layout, and choosing articles and images. Children can be fully involved in the editorial process, for example, by editing articles and proofreading, commissioning work and choosing just the right image for the page. You could hold a weekly meeting with the editorial team and use the school calendar to plan ahead and discuss the types of articles you want in the magazine. Working in collaboration develops team and project management skills. It is a good idea to ask each member of the team to write at least one article for the magazine and, of course, try to include work from as many children in the school as possible.

Resources

- A range of artwork
- Ideas books
- A selection of creative writing, reviews, poetry, artwork

Approach

1 Ask the children to read their magazine articles aloud to the rest of the team for comments.
2 Edit articles with the children on screen with a focus on powerful headlines and use of emotive language.
3 As a group, select photographs that link perfectly with the magazine articles.

Visitors

Inviting speakers to talk to the children about the writing process, or other areas of the Creative Arts is an excellent way to inspire them. For example, ask a journalist to come and speak about the importance of having powerful eye-catching headings for articles, or interview techniques. Children need to be encouraged to take notes during school trips to art galleries or the theatre and then to use their notes as part of the drafting process, in the same way journalists do.

Resources

- Notebooks
- Pencils
- A selection of school magazines
- Camera

Approach

1 Before they meet the school editorial team, explain to visiting speakers exactly what you want them to focus on.
2 Ask the children to prepare a few questions before the visit to ensure a lively session.
3 Encourage the children to take notes during presentations so that feedback sessions are more useful.
4 If you have some printed copies of school magazines, show them to the speakers for comments.
5 Take a photograph of the team with the guest speaker and include it in the magazine.

Everyday Objects

The following drawing activities will help you to develop some creative ways of getting your class to draw from observation. However daunting this task may seem, making drawings from real life remains a fundamental artistic skill which, when introduced well to children, can really promote the act of drawing as an essential life skill.

Step Into It

This is a drawing task using an object that all the children will have on their person. A shoe is a simple form and when observed under bold lighting can introduce the class to the idea of drawing with shading.

Resources

- A shoe
- A3 sketch paper
- Poseable lamp
- Pencils
- Rubber
- Black ink
- Paint brushes
- Water pot
- Sugar paper

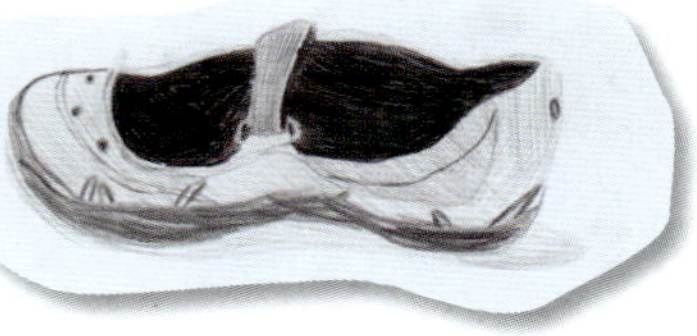

Approach

1 Ask the children to remove one of their shoes and place it in front of them on the table.
2 Give out the paper and drawing pencils. Ask them to draw this outer shape as large as they can.
3 Using the poseable lamp, direct the light down the centre of the table. This should create some real areas of light on dark to help with creating the form of the shoe.
4 Invite the children to fill the form, starting in the darkest area with heavy pencil shading.
5 To create highlights, ask the children to locate the lightest areas and rub out the pencil shading to gain the desired effect.
6 Finally they can use this adding and taking away technique to form detail of lacing, stitching and pattern within the shoe.

Tools for the Job

Pop Artist Jim Dine regularly used the objects around him as inspiration for his work. Many of his observational studies were based on his workshop tools. Focusing on accessible objects in your own classroom is a brilliant way to introduce the children to drawing by encouraging them to see beauty in their immediate surroundings.

Resources

- Tools or classroom equipment
- A3 sketch paper
- Poseable lamp
- Pencils
- Rubber

Approach

1 Begin by either handing out or asking the children to select an object to draw.
2 To help the children build confidence in their use of form in drawing, ask them to draw four small boxes at the top of their sheet of paper.
3 Starting with the box on the left, ask them to shade these boxes with pencil, each one becoming lighter. Children sometimes find it easier to shade the darkest on the left and then the lightest on the right, filling the middle two last.
4 Encourage the children to use these boxes as a key when working on their drawings.
5 The drawing should follow the structure of outline, larger internal shapes, shading and detail. There should be close and constant observation throughout.

'Drawing is not an exercise. Exercise is sitting on a stationary bicycle and going nowhere. Drawing is being on a bicycle and taking a journey. For me to succeed in drawing, I must go fast and arrive somewhere. The quest is to keep the thing alive...'

Jim Dine, 2003

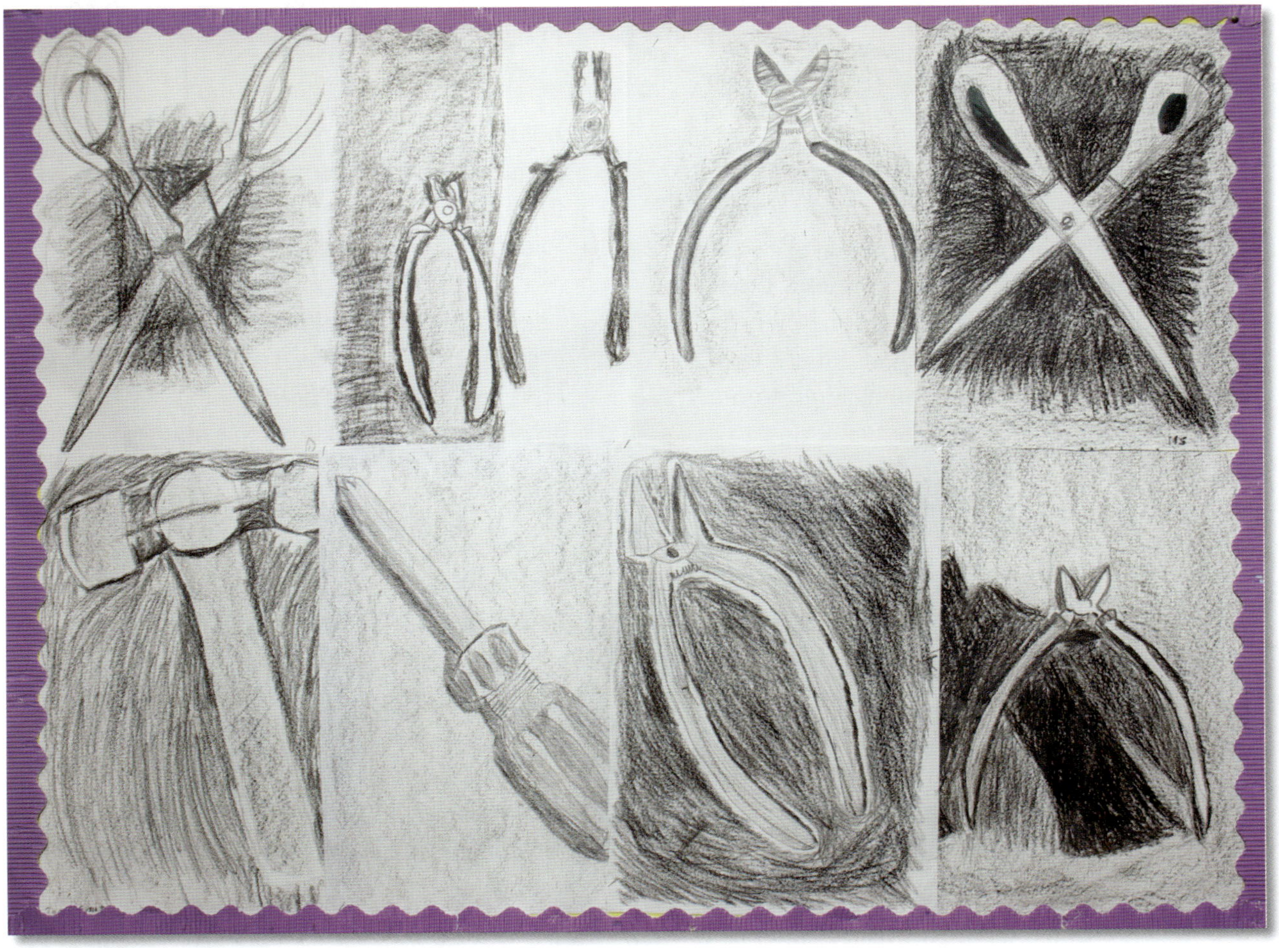

Giant Stationery

The artist Claus Oldenburg took inspiration from everyday objects and produced civic sculptures with a 'parallel reality', where the sculptures become a part of the environment. These giant objects have become bridges, tunnels or roundabouts in cities around the world. By making and then assembling a group of giant stationery objects the children begin to understand the significance of scale and the essential properties these mundane objects possess.

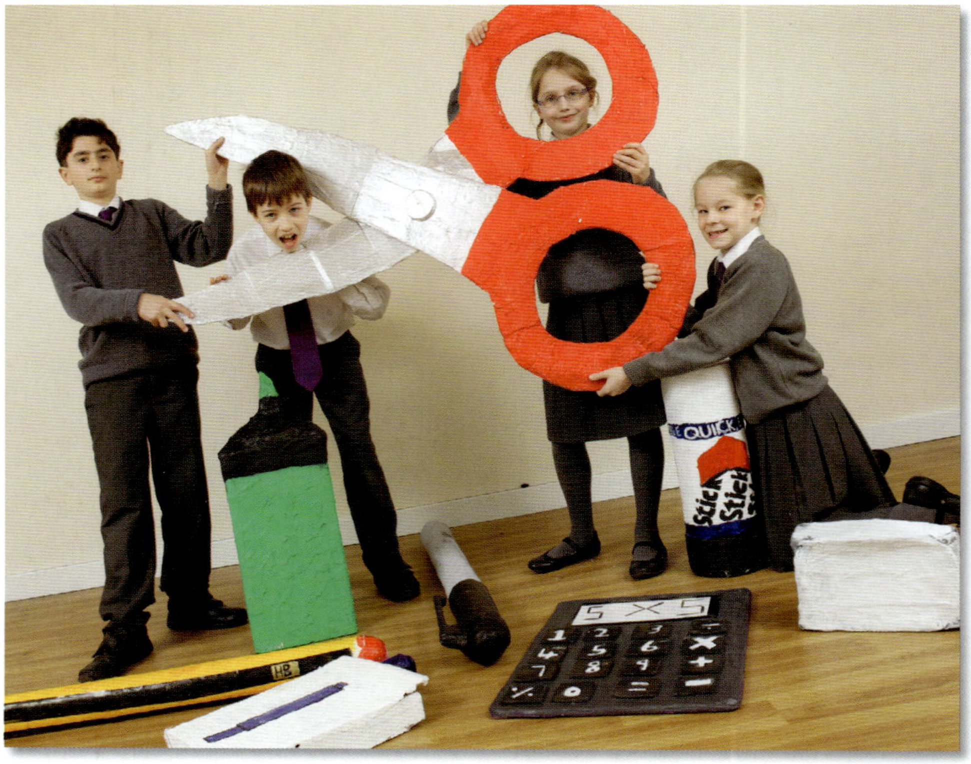

Resources

- Ideas books
- Aprons
- Pencils
- Cardboard
- Scissors
- Masking tape
- Plaster bandage/ Mod-Roc
- Water trays
- Acrylic paint
- Brushes
- Felt pens
- Yacht varnish

Approach

1 Divide the class into groups and hand each group a different piece of stationery to explore. There should be no more than four children working on each sculpture.

2 The initial work for this project takes the form of quick sketches and ideas, done by every member of the group to ensure that they are all contributing. Ask the children to draw the bare bones of the object. Is it one basic shape? Or are there a number of separate shapes to be modelled and fused together?

3 The internal structure of these giant objects is created with simple cardboard framework which can be cut with scissors and secured with masking tape. Adults may need to help with any tricky cutting.

4 Once the internal structure is secure the children can begin to cover it in plaster bandage/Mod-Roc. This can be pre-cut into strips and dipped into the water trays before smoothing straight onto the cardboard surface. The children should use their fingers to smooth down the bandage.

5 Allow around 15 minutes to dry. Whilst waiting, mix appropriate paint colours.

6 Ask the groups to copy any logos or patterns onto their white plaster surfaces with a pencil.

7 Paint the sculptures, carefully matching colours and patterns with the real objects. Leave to dry.

8 The presentation of these sculptures is paramount to the success of this project. They are great to display in a school foyer area or exhibition space. They can be photographed with the children to emphasise their scale, used as props in a school play or with a layer of yacht varnish, can survive many months in an outdoor setting.